PROCRASTINATION

Overcoming the Resistance Within

LEAP Learning Empowerment & Achieving Potential

ISBN 978-93-80154-64-0

First published in 2011 by Leadstart
A brand of One Point Six Technologies Private Limited
Unit no. 26, Ground Floor, A1, Shram Safalya,
Wadala Truck Terminal Road, Near Post Office,
Antop Hill, Mumbai -400037.
Email:info@leadstartcorp.com
www.leadstartcorp.com

Marketed & Distributed in India by Unbound Script
2/41, Ansari Road, Darayaganj, Delhi - 110002

EDITORS OF LEADSTART

The Editors of Leadstart are a team of passionate literary enthusiasts with a creative and progressive focus. Our team includes distinguished authors, researchers, contributors, in-house editors, and writing talent from around the world. Many literary projects require a diverse team rather than a single author to write or update the book. These projects often involve cases where the original author is unable to continue, whether because they are no longer available or have passed away. Our work thus spans a range of content, from original writings to thoughtfully abridged classics, updated editions, and translations.

LEAP Learning Empowerment & Achieving Potential

ABOUT THE LEAP SERIES

The LEAP series of books has been conceived as a tool of empowerment for every individual to achieve their full potential.

There are certain aspirations that every person in the world shares. We all want to be happy. We all want to lead fulfilling lives. We all want to find our soulmate. We all want a job we love doing. We all want good friends who will share our joy and sorrow. We all want to believe that there is a purpose to our lives.

While the commonality of these goals spans the globe, their achievement is entirely individual. Each person possesses a unique and mixed gift of strengths and weaknesses, special talents and handicaps. To focus our individual lives on all that is positive within us, all that is possible for us to do, to be and to achieve, we need to take conscious steps towards it. The empowerment of our lives is an individual pursuit. The decisions are yours. The action is yours. To do the very best with what one has been given – that is the ultimate achievement of a life well lived.

You Are You

First, we must recognise ourselves and accept our particular basket of capabilities. Nobody is the same. Nor is it necessary to be like someone else.

Find Your Horizons

Once we are at peace with the composition of our own individuality, we can set out to enhance our capabilities in order to achieve full potential as an individual. We can utilise all the teaching around us to stretch our talents to the fullest extent to achieve worthwhile goals.

Cap The Leak

Once we recognise our potential, we can work to minimise the influence and impact of our weak points to allow the strengths to shine in everything we do.

Row Your Boat

Every day is part of the journey. Sometimes you win the day. Sometimes the day is lost. But you keep rowing towards the shore, towards your goals. In India, it is called sadhana. That special power within you drives you to achieve what you have set yourself to do.

The LEAP series teaches methods of individual empowerment.

CONTENTS

INTRODUCTION 7

1. The Truth About Procrastination 11
2. Why We Procrastinate: Fear, Fatigue & Fuzzy Goals 15
3. The Real Cost of Delay 19
4. Vision: Fuel with Meaning 24
5. Energy: Build Your Battery 29
6. Focus: Master The Minutes 35
7. The Digital Trap: Reclaiming Your Attention Online 39
8. Ownership: It's On You 44
9. Design for Action 49
10. Face the Real Enemy: Fear 53
11. Emotional Procrastination: When Avoidance Isn't Laziness 57
12. Progress Over Perfection 62
13. Winning Daily: Micro Habits & Goals 67
14. The Momentum Mindset 72
15. How to Keep Going: Resilience & Renewal 76
16. The Accountability Effect 80
17. Helping Others (And Yourself Again) 85

CONCLUSION

The Practice of Progress 90

INTRODUCTION

Procrastination is not a small flaw in productivity. It is one of the most consistent ways human beings limit themselves. It hides behind reasonable excuses, small delays, and temporary distractions, but its effects are profound. It wastes potential, drains confidence, and turns meaningful goals into recurring sources of frustration. It convinces you that waiting will help, when in truth, it builds the habit of postponing what matters most.

Everyone knows what it feels like to delay something important. You promise yourself that you will begin after a break, when the time feels right, or once your energy returns. Yet the longer you wait, the harder it becomes to start. The unfinished work lingers, a weight that follows you through the day. The relief that came with postponing turns into frustration, and that frustration grows into self-doubt. You begin to question your ability to follow through, even when the task itself hasn't changed.

Procrastination is not about laziness. Most people who struggle with it care deeply about their work. They have ambition, ideas, and intent. What they lack is not desire, but control over the forces that shape action. Procrastination begins when emotion overrides purpose. When a task feels uncertain, uncomfortable, or overwhelming, the brain searches for escape. Distraction offers temporary relief, and that relief reinforces avoidance. Over time, this becomes a cycle, an automatic retreat from discomfort that feels logical in the moment, but leaves you further from what you want to achieve.

Breaking that cycle requires clarity, structure, and practice. You do not overcome procrastination through bursts of motivation. You overcome it by understanding how action actually happens, and by strengthening the four inner forces that determine whether you move forward or remain stuck. These forces are Vision, Energy, Focus, and Ownership.

Vision provides direction. It gives shape to your purpose and helps you see where your effort is meant to lead. Without it, even hard work feels scattered and unrewarding.

Energy provides capacity. It fuels the work itself. Without physical vitality and mental clarity, even simple tasks begin to feel like battles. Managing energy, and not just time, is the foundation of sustained progress.

Focus determines the quality of your effort. It turns activity into advancement. In a world built to divide attention, the ability to hold it on one thing has become a rare advantage.

Ownership turns thought into reality. It is the willingness to take responsibility for results. Ownership silences excuses and transforms intention into consistent action.

These four forces form the foundation of this book. Each chapter will show how procrastination weakens them and how deliberate habits can rebuild them. The goal is not to chase perfection but to develop control. To build a relationship with your time, attention, and effort that is sustainable and self-directed. When you understand how these forces work, procrastination stops being a mystery. It becomes a pattern you can interrupt.

We live in an age that rewards constant reaction. Every sound, notification, and message invites your attention elsewhere. The modern worker is surrounded by tools that promise efficiency but often fragment focus instead. The result is a life that feels full of effort but empty of progress. Overcoming procrastination today is not about doing more. It is about reclaiming your capacity to think clearly, choose deliberately, and finish what you start.

You will not learn tricks or shortcuts here. What you will learn is how to work with your own psychology rather than against it; how to reduce the friction between intention and action, how to manage emotion without avoidance, and how to create a rhythm of steady progress that builds confidence over time. You will also learn to recover faster when you fall behind, because lapses are inevitable, but long delays are not.

The purpose of this book is not to make you perfect. It is to make you capable of consistent forward motion. The ability to act, even when conditions are not ideal, is one of the strongest predictors of success in any field. You do not need to wait for inspiration or certainty. You need to begin, learn from movement itself, and refine as you go.

Change begins when you stop negotiating with delay. Every moment you spend waiting is one you could spend building. You already can act with focus and intention. This book will show you how to use it.

Let's begin.

ᘓᘐ

1

THE TRUTH ABOUT PROCRASTINATION

Procrastination is not simply a delay in action. It is a convincing illusion that persuades you to wait, whispering that more time will make things easier, that you will be better prepared tomorrow, or that a brief rest will help you begin with renewed strength. Yet procrastination feeds on postponement. The longer you wait, the heavier the task becomes, and what once required a single act of effort begins to demand endurance.

Most people who procrastinate are not lazy. In fact, they often care deeply about the things they avoid. They want to do them well, so well, in fact, that the fear of falling short stops them from beginning at all. The gap between intention and action becomes a place of hesitation, filled with preparation, planning, and endless refinement that leads nowhere. Procrastination thrives in that gap. Each moment of hesitation strengthens its grip, and what feels like preparation is often a form of avoidance disguised as diligence.

At its core, procrastination is not a problem of time management but of emotion. The mind attempts to protect itself from discomfort. When a task stirs self-doubt, fear, or uncertainty, the brain looks for a quick escape. It finds relief in distraction: checking messages, rearranging a desk, and refreshing a page. These actions offer the illusion of productivity, but they slowly weaken confidence. Each time you choose distraction over discomfort, you train your mind to equate relief with safety. The next time resistance appears, the same pattern repeats automatically, and the habit deepens.

This cycle gives procrastination its power. Every postponed action strengthens the association between effort and unease. Over time, the hardest part of any task becomes the act of starting. What we mistake for a lack of time is often a reluctance to face discomfort. The true challenge is not in managing hours but in managing emotion, to move forward even when the mind urges to retreat.

Procrastination also survives on the illusion of later. The mind insists that waiting will help you prepare, that you will feel stronger, clearer, or more inspired tomorrow. Yet delay does not renew energy. Each day spent postponing adds mental weight to the task and erodes the will to begin. Soon, even thinking about the work feels more exhausting than the work itself.

Breaking this pattern begins with motion. You do not wait for readiness; readiness grows from movement. Progress begins in the smallest of acts, like writing one sentence, opening the document, or making a single call. These first steps teach the brain that effort is manageable and momentum is possible. The moment you start, your perception shifts: the task shrinks, and confidence begins to return. You create progress not by completing everything at once but by proving to yourself that forward motion is still within your control.

Enthusiasm strengthens this process. Thomas Edison once called enthusiasm a quality of incalculable value. When his laboratory burned down, destroying years of work, he did not collapse into despair. Instead, he called his family to watch the fire and began rebuilding within days. His reaction was not blind optimism; it was a deliberate choice to stay engaged. He understood that energy follows involvement, not discouragement. Enthusiasm is not a burst of emotion that arrives when conditions are perfect; it is a perspective you choose to maintain when they are not.

You can choose it, too. Enthusiasm is not a feeling you wait for but a discipline you practice. When you meet resistance with engagement instead of avoidance, you turn effort into energy. The moment you begin, the very act of working generates the drive you thought you were missing. Momentum is not the result of motivation, but the source of it.

When you notice yourself slipping into delay, shift your focus to one tangible action. Choose a specific task and begin, even if only for a short time. Identify when your mind is at its sharpest and schedule your most demanding work for that window. Protect that time from unnecessary interruptions and environments that weaken your focus. Each time you complete what you have been avoiding, you build a small but significant proof of ability. Progress in one area restores energy in others. And when the work flows easily, pay attention to why. Notice the time, the place, and the mindset that made it possible, and rebuild those conditions whenever you can.

Mark Twain once wrote, "Do something every day that you do not want to do." It is a simple idea, but it contains the essence of discipline. Consistent follow-through builds trust in your own ability to act. Discipline is not formed through grand achievements but through the steady practice of effort without negotiation. Each time you complete what you resisted, you teach yourself that discomfort can be endured and that progress is possible even without perfect conditions. Confidence grows not from wishing but from evidence, and that evidence is created through doing.

Procrastination loses its strength when you stop believing its most convincing lie, that later will be easier. Later never is. The only moment that carries power is the one in front of you. The instant you begin, the weight of avoidance begins to lift. You reclaim your time, your energy, and your peace of mind. You remember that effort is not the enemy of ease; it is the path to it.

ꕥ

2

WHY WE PROCRASTINATE

Fear, Fatigue & Fuzzy Goals

Procrastination rarely begins with disinterest. It begins with hesitation, the pause before movement when your mind whispers, *not yet*. It convinces you that another moment of rest, one more round of preparation, or a clearer mood will make beginning easier. That voice feels protective, but it is not. It is resistance disguised as reason. Beneath that hesitation lie deeper roots: fear, fatigue, and the fog of unclear goals.

We often believe procrastination is a failure of time management, but it is far more a failure of emotional management. You are not avoiding the task itself; you are avoiding the feelings the task provokes. Some tasks carry the weight of uncertainty or the risk of failure. Others awaken perfectionism or self-doubt. The mind, seeking relief, redirects you toward comfort, towards scrolling, cleaning, checking messages, small actions that feel harmless but pull you further from your intention. Each act of avoidance provides a momentary calm while reinforcing the idea that escape equals safety.

Fear is the most persistent cause of delay. It hides behind rational language and admirable intentions. It tells you that you need more time, more research, or better conditions before beginning. It whispers that patience is prudence, when in truth, it is protection from vulnerability. Fear of failure argues that not trying is safer than trying and falling short. Fear of judgment says that invisibility protects you from criticism. Even fear of success can hold you back, warning that achievement will bring new expectations you might not be ready to meet. None of these fears is inherently truthful, yet they feel convincing because they sound responsible. You mistake hesitation for preparation when it is really avoidance in disguise.

Then there is fatigue. When your mind and body are exhausted, resistance grows stronger. You tell yourself you are too tired to begin, when in reality, beginning would restore some of the very energy you lack. Mental fatigue builds over time through overcommitment, emotional strain, and endless stimulation. Every unfinished thought becomes an open loop your brain must hold. You may seek escape through passive rest, such as scrolling, snacking, and watching, but those activities rarely replenish energy. They numb the discomfort without resolving it. Real restoration comes from rhythm, not retreat: cycles of focused effort followed by deliberate recovery. The people who sustain progress are not those who never tire, but those who know how to renew themselves before depletion turns into paralysis.

And sometimes, what holds you back is not fear or fatigue, but confusion. You cannot direct energy toward what you cannot define. When goals are vague, action feels uncertain. You might promise yourself you will "get organised," "be healthier," or "focus more," but without a clear definition of success, the mind resists movement. It does not know where to aim. Clarity is the antidote. The clearer your direction, the lighter the first step becomes. The brain thrives on precision, and it needs to know what to do next, not simply what to want.

Consider Tanya, a designer known for her creativity and ideas. She carried a notebook filled with sketches and plans for her dream brand, and her friends often called her a visionary. Yet despite her talent, months passed, and her dream remained on paper. Each time she sat down to start, tension built in her chest. She feared that her work would not be good enough, that others would not take her seriously, that the result would fall short of her vision. So she kept researching, adjusting fonts, and collecting inspiration. She stayed busy but not productive. She mistook movement for progress.

One evening, she asked herself a simple question: "What am I afraid might happen if I start?" Her answer came quickly, "People might think it isn't good enough." Then she asked, "What will happen if I keep waiting?" That answer was harder: "Nothing." That night, she built a single-page website and shared a design. It was not perfect, but it was real. Within days, she received her first message from a client. Nothing magical had changed in her ability—only her willingness to begin. Once she saw that nothing catastrophic followed her action, her fear began to lose authority. She learned that courage is not the absence of fear, but the refusal to let fear decide.

Fear, fatigue, and fuzzy goals take different shapes, but they lead to the same result: stagnation. They shield you from discomfort while costing you long-term confidence. The cure for all three begins with awareness. Fear weakens when you expose it to truth. Fatigue recedes when you restore balance instead of seeking escape. Unclear goals solidify when you translate them into concrete steps. Awareness transforms hesitation into understanding, and understanding creates space for choice.

If there is something you have been postponing, pause and look closer. Ask yourself what is truly stopping you. Write down the answers. Then challenge them. What are you afraid might happen if you begin? What is more likely to happen if you continue to wait? Seeing both on paper exposes the gap between perception and fact. It is rarely the task itself that frightens us, but the imagined consequence that never arrives.

You do not have to feel fearless to act. You only have to stop treating hesitation as a command to retreat. Progress does not wait for confidence; confidence grows out of progress. Each time you act despite uncertainty, you strengthen the part of yourself that leads. Fear begins to lose its authority, fatigue loosens its grip, and your goals gain definition through movement.

You may never find the perfect moment to begin, but the act of beginning creates its own conditions. Once you stop waiting for the right time, you discover that the right time was always the moment you decided to move.

ꕥ

3

THE REAL COST OF DELAY

Procrastination carries a cost that extends far deeper than most people realise. It does not simply steal time; it drains your energy, weakens your confidence, and erodes your sense of control over your own life. Every task you delay grows heavier in your mind, not because the work itself changes, but because avoidance multiplies its weight. A task that might have taken half an hour yesterday begins to feel like a mountain today. The burden lies not in the doing but in the constant awareness that it remains undone. What exhausts you is the strain of carrying something unfinished in your thoughts while trying to move forward with everything else.

William James once wrote that nothing is as fatiguing as the hanging weight of an uncompleted task. He was describing the mental drag of unfinished work, and the way it lingers at the edge of your consciousness, even when you think you've put it aside. You might be at dinner, or trying to rest, or halfway through another project, and the reminder slips in: *you still haven't done it*. It's rarely loud or urgent, but it's always there, whispering through moments that should belong to peace or presence. Over time, this creates what psychologists call "mental load," the accumulation of small, unresolved obligations that scatter attention and sap emotional energy.

The longer a task remains undone, the more attention it demands. The mind keeps a running list of open loops, unfinished actions that need closure, and each one takes up a portion of your mental bandwidth. Even when you aren't consciously thinking about them, they occupy space. You may find yourself restless, distracted, unable to relax, and you can't quite explain why. The truth is, every incomplete task you carry acts like an anchor, tethering your focus to the past and your energy to indecision. The longer you wait, the heavier the chain becomes.

Procrastination thrives in this tension. Each delay sends a message to your subconscious: *I can't trust myself to act right now.* You don't mean to believe it, but the repetition builds the association. What starts as hesitation soon reshapes your self-image. You begin to see yourself as someone who struggles to start, someone who cannot quite follow through. This belief is the most damaging part of procrastination, not the time lost, but the erosion of faith in your own dependability. The mind learns from evidence, and when the evidence says you hesitate more often than you act, confidence begins to slip away.

Ironically, procrastination never gives the comfort it promises. Waiting does not make the work easier. It merely makes it heavier. The task does not shrink while you ignore it; it grows in your imagination until it feels impossible. What might have been resolved in minutes begins to feel like a test of your entire ability. The weight of indecision often becomes far more exhausting than the effort of completion itself. And so, without realising it, you spend more energy avoiding the task than you ever would have spent doing it.

The cure is not more planning or perfect timing. It is an action. The moment you begin, no matter how small the step, the burden starts to lift. Action releases the energy that hesitation has trapped. One email sent, one form filled, one call made, and the pressure begins to ease. The fog clears. Progress, even minimal progress, breaks the illusion of impossibility. The mind's confidence returns because it finally has evidence of forward motion. Confidence does not come from thinking about success; it comes from proving to yourself that you can move even through resistance.

Many people confuse movement with progress. They fill their days with motion, such as checking messages, responding to emails, rearranging their schedules, attending meetings, and call it productivity. But none of it moves the needle where it matters. Busyness offers the comfort of activity without the discomfort of risk. You feel as though you're working hard, yet by nightfall, the most important thing remains untouched. This is the trap of false progress. It gives the illusion of control while perpetuating the very cycle of delay it seeks to avoid.

To break that illusion, you must first become aware of how you spend your time. Try documenting a single day without judgment. Write down each activity, however small, and note how long it takes. When you review it, you will begin to see how much of your energy is lost in fragments, moments of distraction, repetition, or avoidance disguised as preparation. Procrastination rarely hides in grand gestures; it lives in these small, harmless-seeming pauses that stretch endlessly. Awareness is the first act of discipline. Once you see where your time goes, you can decide, with intention, how to reclaim it.

The next step is structure. Clear goals dissolve confusion, and confusion is the soil in which procrastination grows. When you do not define what matters, everything competes for your attention. A vague goal like "work on the project" is a recipe for distraction; a specific goal like "draft the first paragraph of the proposal by noon" gives the mind a target. You do not need to plan your entire journey before starting. Only the next step that matters. Structure reduces resistance because it removes ambiguity, and ambiguity is what the mind resists most.

Time does not pause while you hesitate. Every hour spent waiting is an hour surrendered to uncertainty. This truth is not meant to shame you but to awaken you to what is still possible. The hours you have lost to hesitation are not beyond recovery. They can be redeemed through deliberate, consistent movement. Each time you turn intention into action, you reclaim a piece of yourself from the inertia of delay. Each time you begin, you reinforce the truth that momentum is always available.

Action is the only cure for procrastination because it dissolves the very conditions that sustain it. When you move, you stop negotiating with fear. You remind yourself that effort is temporary while avoidance lasts indefinitely. Every task you finish returns a measure of calm to your mind. You learn that starting is not as painful as the anticipation of starting, and that completion restores a kind of power, the peace that comes from keeping your word to yourself.

The true cost of delay is invisible until you look closely. It starts as unease, then grows into self-doubt, then into the loss of confidence that limits what you attempt next. Its toll is not measured in hours, but in opportunities unclaimed and energy wasted on hesitation. You pay for it every day you choose inaction over effort. Yet the solution is beautifully simple. Movement restores energy. Action rebuilds confidence. The decision to begin reclaiming time. Each time you act, you close one open loop and strengthen the habit of progress. You cannot control how much time you have, but you can control what you do with it, and that choice, made again and again, is what separates a life lived in motion from one lived in momentum.

ഇര

4

VISION

Fuel with Meaning

When you move through life without a clear sense of direction, every demand feels urgent, yet nothing feels meaningful. You may work hard and stay busy, but your energy disperses because it has no central aim. Tasks compete for your attention, priorities blur, and your actions begin to lose coherence. This is the condition in which procrastination thrives. It is not always born of laziness or fear; sometimes it is the natural consequence of moving without orientation. When you do not know where you are going, distractions appear reasonable. When you do not know why you are going, every step feels heavy. Vision restores both. It gives structure to your energy, order to your ambition, and purpose to your effort.

A powerful vision is not a burst of inspiration or a motivational slogan taped to a wall. It is a continuous act of alignment between what matters most to you and how you live each day. Vision is clarity that guides action. It shapes how you spend your time, whom you listen to, and which opportunities you pursue. When your vision is clear, you no longer wait for motivation to appear. The direction itself begins to generate momentum. You move because meaning pulls you forward. Work that once felt like an obligation becomes an expression of intention. You stop trying to create discipline through pressure and instead sustain it through purpose.

Every significant human achievement begins with such clarity. Edison's vision of light extended beyond invention; it was about illuminating lives. Walt Disney imagined not merely an amusement park but a living world of imagination. Martin Luther King Jr. carried a vision of a nation transformed by justice and character. None of these figures acted out of temporary motivation. They acted out of conviction, a steady image of what could exist if they persisted. Vision does not eliminate struggle, but it transforms struggle into progress. It allows you to interpret obstacles as part of the path instead of as signs to turn back.

When people say they lack motivation, what they often lack is direction. You cannot sustain commitment to something you only vaguely understand. Goals like "be successful" or "get healthier" are too abstract to generate energy. The mind cannot act with power on a blurry idea. It needs a tangible image of what success looks and feels like. That image must connect both intellectually and emotionally, because emotion provides the fuel that logic alone cannot. Once that picture is formed, even small steps begin to matter. Each act of effort becomes a piece of a larger pattern, and the sense of progress itself becomes motivating.

Clarity also protects you from pursuing ambitions that are not truly yours. Many people spend years chasing goals they inherited, from parents, peers, or the culture around them, only to find that reaching them feels hollow. You can achieve everything society calls success and still feel lost if the vision behind that success does not belong to you. Energy fades when purpose does not align with identity. True vision grows from within. It emerges from your values, your experiences, and your sense of what gives life meaning. When your choices reflect your principles, you draw strength from your actions rather than spending it. Effort becomes easier to sustain because it expresses who you are rather than who you think you should be.

Building that kind of vision begins not with planning but with reflection. Before asking what you want to accomplish, ask who you wish to become. Think about what kind of person you admire most and what qualities in them you wish to cultivate in yourself. Consider how you want your daily life to feel, what balance of work, growth, and relationships would make you feel grounded and alive. Reflect on what kind of work makes you feel capable and fulfilled rather than depleted, and what kind of relationships mirror the values you hold most dear. These questions are not meant to be answered quickly. They are meant to clarify what already calls to you beneath the noise of daily demands. Vision begins when you start listening to your own inner direction.

Once that clarity takes shape, decision-making changes. Choices that once felt complex become simple. You stop scattering effort because you can now measure each opportunity against a single, steady question: *Does this bring me closer to the life I want to build, or does it pull me further away?* This becomes a compass. It replaces the anxious need to evaluate every option with the confidence of knowing what aligns and what does not. When your time and attention begin to follow your vision, distractions lose their grip. You no longer need to chase every opportunity or prove yourself through endless activity. You move deliberately, spending energy only where it amplifies your direction.

A person guided by vision does not live reactively. They move through the world with awareness, understanding that every decision builds toward something greater. They are not waiting for perfect conditions or sudden bursts of inspiration. Their steadiness comes from alignment. When effort serves a meaningful purpose, it begins to sustain itself. Motivation no longer depends on mood because the work has been integrated into identity. You act not to avoid guilt but to fulfil a promise, to yourself and to what you stand for.

This is the power of vision. It transforms activity into purpose and converts habit into intention. It brings coherence to the scattered noise of modern life. It does not erase difficulty, but it allows you to face difficulty with understanding. When you know what you are working toward, you stop asking whether the struggle is worth it. The meaning itself becomes the answer. Vision links the present to the future, giving continuity to your days and context to your challenges.

You do not need to see your vision in full to begin living it. Vision evolves through action. It becomes clearer each time you make a choice that reflects your values and each time you step toward something that feels authentic. As your actions align with your convictions, your confidence in your direction deepens. This alignment becomes resilience.

Even when conditions change, your sense of purpose remains stable because it is anchored in clarity rather than circumstance.

Living with vision does not mean having every detail planned. It means knowing enough about what matters to act with intention today. It means measuring your progress not by speed but by direction. When vision leads, procrastination begins to lose its grip. The uncertainty that once invited delay is replaced by a meaning that invites motion. You stop moving out of obligation and start moving out of conviction. Purpose replaces pressure. Direction replaces doubt.

A person who lives with vision lives deliberately. They are not pulled by every distraction or exhausted by every demand. Their actions gather momentum because they are all pointed toward something coherent and chosen. Vision does not just give you goals. It gives you a way to live. It turns each day into a step in a larger story, one in which even the smallest effort matters. And that, more than anything else, is what frees you from delay.

ꕥ

5

ENERGY

Build Your Battery

You can have the clearest goals, the most disciplined plan, and the strongest intentions, but without energy, nothing moves. Energy is the foundation of action. It determines how much you can do, how deeply you can think, and how steadily you can persist when work stretches longer than expected. When your energy is full, effort feels natural and focus comes easily. Ideas connect, decisions feel cleaner, and you can hold your attention on a single path without constantly fighting yourself. When energy runs low, even a simple task can feel impossible. Your thinking narrows, your patience thins, and starting begins to feel like lifting a weight that will not budge.

Most people who delay do not lack ambition. They are worn down. They wake already tense, step into a stream of alerts and requests, and spend their day reacting. By evening, they are mentally spent but strangely unsatisfied, because a day consumed by reaction yields little that feels meaningful. This is the paradox of modern work:

you can expend enormous effort and still feel as though you have not moved. In that state, the brain seeks relief, not progress. It grabs for what is easy and immediately comforting, and the longer this pattern continues, the more convincing it becomes. You tell yourself you will begin when you have more drive, yet drive rarely appears without a change in energy. The first step is to treat energy as a resource that can be built, protected, and directed, rather than something that arrives or disappears by chance.

Modern life drains energy in ways that feel trivial in the moment but cumulative across a day. Each notification prompts a decision. Each tab left open represents a task your mind must track. Even short exchanges can leave residue, because your attention must detach and reattach each time. These micro costs add up to real fatigue. Leisure that is packed with stimulation gives the illusion of rest while producing more mental clutter. You close your laptop but keep scrolling, and the brain never fully unwinds. Reclaiming energy begins with subtraction. Fewer simultaneous inputs allow the nervous system to settle. A simpler desk, a pared-down set of tools, and a clear entry point for the next session of work remove friction before it forms. Energy saved on reorienting is energy available for thinking.

Movement is the fastest, honest way to change your state. Human physiology is designed for action, and thought becomes clearer when the body participates. You do not need long sessions or elaborate routines to benefit. A brisk ten-minute walk can refocus attention. A set of stretches between meetings can lower tension in the shoulders and back, which in turn reduces the background noise of discomfort that competes with your thoughts. Strength training teaches the brain to meet rising effort with composed breathing rather than panic. Interval work teaches recovery on demand. These are not merely fitness outcomes. They are cognitive benefits delivered through the body. When movement is part of your day, you create more chances to feel capable, and capability is energising.

Energy also depends on rhythm. Muscles grow during recovery, and attention behaves similarly. The mind performs best when it cycles between depth and renewal. Long, uninterrupted sprints without recovery degrade output and tempt escape. Short, intense blocks paired with real rest preserve sharpness. The length of the block matters less than the integrity of the boundary. During work, protect a single objective. During recovery, protect the right to step away. Pauses should replenish, not distract. A walk outdoors, a glass of water in a different room, a few pages of a book that steadies the mind, or two minutes of deliberate breathing will refuel better than aimless scrolling that fractures attention and leaves you starting over when you return. Sleep sits at the centre of this rhythm. It consolidates memory, regulates emotion, and restores the systems that allow for decisive action. Treating sleep as negotiable is a tax on every hour that follows.

What you consume becomes how you think. Food that spikes and crashes your blood sugar sets up mood swings that feel like motivation problems. Heavy meals at the wrong time invite lethargy just when you intend to do focused work. Hydration affects cognition more than most people realise; a slight deficit reduces processing speed and increases irritability, both of which feed delay. Caffeine is a useful tool when paired with timing and restraint, but it cannot compensate for chronic sleep debt, and overuse creates a cycle of stimulation followed by depletion that leaves you chasing equilibrium. Even breathing patterns shape energy. Shallow chest breathing signals stress to the body and narrows attention to threats. Slow, steady breaths through the nose tell the nervous system that effort is safe, which widens attention and makes complex work feel manageable. None of this requires perfection. Small, repeatable improvements change how a day feels.

Your environment either leaks energy or returns it. Clutter forces the brain to filter irrelevant details before it finds the relevant ones. Constant background noise raises the internal volume of your thoughts. Tools with endless features invite tinkering when you intend to execute. A clean physical setup, a default document that opens to the current project, and boundaries around communication windows are not aesthetic choices. They are energy policies. They reduce the cost of starting and the temptation to drift. The goal is not sterility. The goal is intentionality, so that the world around you supports the work in front of you.

Perspective converts the same effort into a different experience. When you interpret work as an imposition, your body tightens, your mind resists, and your energy drains before you begin. When you interpret the same work as a chance to build competence, to contribute, or to honour a value you chose, you regain authority over your effort. Gratitude is often misunderstood as decoration for good days, when in practice it is leverage for hard days. Remembering that you are healthy enough to work, trusted enough to be asked, and equipped enough to make a difference does not erase difficulty. It reminds you why the difficulty is worth meeting. That reminder restores energy without a nap or a snack, because meaning is fuel.

Discipline is the bridge between energy and results. Motivation fluctuates. Discipline allows you to begin anyway. Each time you start in the absence of enthusiasm, you teach your nervous system that discomfort can coexist with forward motion. The lesson compounds. You argue with yourself less. You spend less time negotiating and more time doing. This is not a call to grind without sense. It is an invitation to build a default response: when in doubt, take the first concrete step. Open the file. Draft the outline. Prepare the tools. After that first inch, momentum often takes over. The act of engaging produces the sensation of readiness you thought you needed before you could engage.

Many people believe energy must arrive before action. Professionals in demanding fields learn a different sequence. They act first, and the act produces energy. This principle is visible in physical training, in creative practice, and in leadership. The warmup precedes the performance not only to prevent injury but to wake up the system. In life, the warm-up can be as simple as five minutes committed to the next piece of the work. If you feel resistance, shrink the step until it is beneath the threshold of avoidance, then move. You will often find that what felt like a wall was only inertia. Once in motion, resistance loses its authority.

Managing energy is a form of maturity. It means you understand your personal patterns and design your days accordingly. It means you respect limits without using them as excuses. It means you give effort to what matters most when your capacity is highest and save administrative tasks for lower peaks. It means you can press when the situation calls for it and recover when the cost would not be repaid. It means you see your mind and body as one system and choose in ways that help that system function at its best.

Energy is finite within a day but renewable across days. It grows with care, rhythm, and purpose. The more consistently you protect it, the more naturally it returns. You will still have heavy weeks and imperfect days. What changes is your default. You stop treating energy as a mystery and start treating it as something you cultivate. When you do, energy becomes more than fuel. It becomes presence. It is the ability to show up with attention, steadiness, and strength, to give your work and your relationships the best of you rather than what remains after distraction.

Do not wait to feel transformed. Begin where you are. Walk around the block to reset your mind. Clear the desk and open the document that matters. Choose a bedtime and keep it. Eat to think rather than to numb. Breathe in a way that supports effort. Treat movement as nonnegotiable. Interpret your work as a privilege rather than a punishment. Start small and let momentum do part of the lifting. Each of these choices is simple. Together, they build a battery that holds a charge. And once you carry that charge into your day, procrastination loses one of its most reliable allies.

ജ്ജ

6

FOCUS

Master The Minutes

Focus is the difference between movement and progress. You can fill a day with activity and still accomplish nothing if your attention is scattered. In a world that constantly demands your eyes, ears, and thoughts, focus has become one of the rarest and most valuable abilities a person can cultivate. It is not intensity alone that creates results, but also the ability to direct that intensity toward one thing long enough for it to matter.

Most people underestimate how fragile attention really is. Each time you check your phone, glance at a notification, or switch tabs, the mind pays a tax. It must pause, reorient, and rebuild the thread of thought it abandoned. Do this a few dozen times in an hour, and the mind becomes frayed, unable to hold an idea from beginning to end. You may feel busy, but busyness is not the same as focus. Busyness scatters; focus consolidates. When you work in a focused state, time compresses. Hours can pass without friction. Distraction, by contrast, stretches time painfully thin. Minutes feel longer because progress is shorter.

Focus is not a gift that some people are born with. It is a discipline anyone can develop. The first step is learning to set priorities. When everything feels urgent, the mind becomes anxious, darting from one unfinished thought to another. You begin to react to noise instead of responding to purpose. The cure for this is selection. Identify what matters most, write it down, and commit to it fully for a fixed period. Clarity reduces chaos. When you decide what not to do, you reclaim energy for what truly deserves it.

The second step is to structure your time in ways that protect attention from being diluted. The brain works best in rhythms of focus and release. A task that seems overwhelming when imagined in full becomes manageable when divided into specific blocks. Assign yourself a single objective for each block of time, begin with a clear starting action, and stop when the time is done. The value of this method is not only in the work completed but in the mental boundary it creates. You learn that focus has edges, that attention, once confined, gains power.

Distraction is the enemy of deep thought. It does not always look like chaos; sometimes it wears the disguise of minor productivity. Checking email, reorganising notes, or browsing for inspiration all feel useful, but they erode momentum. True focus requires a deliberate environment. Silence notifications, close what is unrelated, and keep only what serves the task in front of you. If your surroundings cannot be fully controlled, use headphones or background sound that drowns external noise without dividing your attention. Over time, your mind will learn to associate this environment with deep engagement. Even a small ritual, like the same chair, the same playlist, at a particular time of day, can signal the brain that it is time to enter the zone.

This is the essence of deep work. It is not simply long hours but full presence. It is the sustained immersion that allows complex thoughts to unfold. The first minutes of deep work often feel uncomfortable. You will want to check something, stretch, or escape. Stay through that threshold. On the other side lies a state where effort feels natural and ideas begin to flow. Each time you practice reaching this state, you strengthen the pathways that allow you to return faster next time. Focus grows through repetition, just like strength.

Time boxing is one of the simplest and most effective tools to train this habit. Choose a single task, set a timer, and commit to working without interruption until it ends. The aim is not perfection or completion; it is presence. The timer creates both a boundary and a promise. For that period, your task has your full allegiance. When it ends, stop, rest, and evaluate. Over time, this rhythm of focus and release builds momentum. It also teaches you that motivation is not a prerequisite for action. You do not wait to feel ready; you begin, and readiness follows.

Focus is also strengthened by awareness of your natural cycles. Every person has hours of peak clarity and hours when the mind dulls. Protect your high-energy windows for your most demanding work and schedule lighter, administrative tasks for the valleys. This alignment of effort and energy produces disproportionate results. Working in harmony with your biology is far more efficient than forcing productivity against it.

To master focus, you must also redefine success. It is not about constant productivity or unbroken concentration. It is about returning to the task each time your attention drifts. The measure of focus is not how rarely you are distracted, but how quickly you recover. Distractions are inevitable; discipline is optional. The simple act of noticing you have wandered and bringing yourself back is what builds the mental muscle of concentration. Each return is a repetition that strengthens your ability to hold attention longer next time.

The modern world is engineered to fracture attention. Every platform, message, and sound competes for your mental bandwidth. To live with focus is to live against this current. It requires intentional resistance. But the reward is extraordinary: when you learn to control your attention, you regain ownership of your time. You begin to experience the satisfaction that comes not from doing more, but from doing with depth.

Focus is not a constant state; it is a practised art of return. You build it through structure, awareness, and repetition. Protect your attention as you would any valuable resource, because it is one. Each moment you spend in full concentration refines your ability to live deliberately. And once you master your minutes, you begin to master your life.

ꙮ

7

THE DIGITAL TRAP

Reclaiming Your Attention Online

Modern procrastination wears a sleek disguise. It no longer looks like idleness; it looks like scrolling, checking, refreshing, and reacting. The digital world offers constant engagement but little fulfilment, infinite information but minimal reflection. You sit down to begin one task and, before you realise it, an hour has vanished into a blur of notifications and noise. What once required deliberate effort, like finding news, connecting with people, and seeking entertainment, is now delivered in endless streams that demand nothing but attention. In that stream, your focus dissolves. The modern mind is not exhausted by work; it is exhausted by distraction.

The internet has redefined how attention is spent. Every notification is an invitation to redirect focus, every feed a system designed to hold you just long enough to forget what you meant to do. These tools are not neutral. They are engineered to harvest time by exploiting the brain's reward mechanisms. Each alert, like a slot machine pull, offers the possibility of something new, a message, or, like a piece of news, something that feels meaningful for a moment before fading. Over time, this cycle rewires the brain to crave stimulation over substance. You begin to check, not because you need to, but because you cannot not check. Procrastination has become less about avoidance and more about addiction to novelty.

Awareness is the first act of freedom. You cannot reclaim what you do not notice. Begin by observing your habits without judgment. Notice when your hand reaches for the phone. Notice what you feel before you open an app—boredom, uncertainty, fatigue. Often, what you are seeking is not information but relief from discomfort. The urge to check is the modern form of escape, a brief way to step away from a task that feels difficult, uncertain, or emotionally demanding. But that relief carries a hidden cost. Each glance fractures focus, and fractured focus cannot produce depth.

Attention behaves like a muscle; each interruption weakens its endurance. Studies show that after a single distraction, it can take over twenty minutes for the brain to return to its previous level of concentration. Multiply that by dozens of interruptions across a day, and you begin to see why modern work feels so fragmented. The hours may be long, but the depth is thin. Reclaiming focus is not about rejecting technology. It is about using it consciously rather than being used by it.

To begin reclaiming attention, you must reestablish boundaries between online noise and deliberate use. Design your digital environment to reduce temptation before it arises. Turn off nonessential notifications. Move distracting apps from your home screen. Keep your phone in another room during deep work sessions. Small physical barriers create a large psychological distance. Each layer of friction restores a measure of control. You are no longer constantly reacting; you are choosing when to engage.

Equally important is defining the purpose of your online time before you begin. The difference between distraction and use lies in intention. Open a browser with a question, not curiosity, without direction. Decide in advance what you are looking for, how long you will spend, and what you will do afterwards. This simple practice converts technology from a source of impulse into a tool of execution. When the task is complete, step away. Closing the loop trains the brain to associate online activity with purpose rather than endless wandering.

Your digital habits mirror your inner state. When you feel uncertain, you search. When you feel disconnected, you scroll. When you feel anxious, you refresh. Recognising this link helps you address the cause instead of the symptom. Ask yourself what emotion you are avoiding each time you reach for a distraction. Often, the answer reveals what truly needs your attention: fatigue that needs rest, fear that needs courage, and confusion that needs clarity. By facing the feeling directly, you dissolve the need to escape from it digitally.

True focus cannot coexist with constant stimulation. Depth requires space. Mental, emotional, and temporal. To reclaim that space, you must practice periods of deliberate disconnection. Schedule specific windows where you are unreachable, even briefly. Protect them as you would a meeting with your most important client. During those times, let your mind reaccustom itself to stillness. Walk without headphones. Work with your phone out of sight. Let thoughts unfold without interruption. In those moments, you recover the ability to think in full sentences rather than fragments.

The digital world rewards reaction. Real life rewards reflection. The more time you spend responding to what others post, the less time you have to create something of your own. Your energy follows your attention, and attention spent in fragments cannot build anything lasting. Choose creation over consumption at least once a day. Write instead of scrolling. Read deeply instead of skimming. Reach out to one person directly instead of broadcasting to many anonymously. Each of these choices strengthens the habit of presence over passivity.

None of this requires rejection of technology; it requires mastery of it. Technology expands human capacity when governed by intention and limits it when allowed to rule attention. You are not powerless in this exchange. You decide when to engage, what to consume, and how to interpret the noise that surrounds you. The act of deciding is itself a reclaiming of strength.

The digital trap is not only about time lost; it is about depth forfeited. The constant stream of stimulation conditions you to live on the surface of things, and to skim rather than absorb, to react rather than reflect. Over time, this surface living dulls curiosity, empathy, and patience, the very qualities that make learning and connection meaningful. To reclaim your attention online is to reclaim these human capacities. It is important to remember that your worth is not measured by visibility, that your peace does not depend on updates, and that silence is not the absence of connection but the space where thought matures.

Procrastination today is rarely about doing nothing. It is about doing everything except what matters. The modern challenge is not to fill time but to focus it. Reclaiming your attention online is not a withdrawal from the world, but instead, a return to yourself. When you learn to direct your attention deliberately, the same tools that once drained you become instruments of creation. You regain the ability to think deeply, work steadily, and rest fully. And in that state, you rediscover something most people have lost: the simple power of being fully present in your own life.

ꙮ

8

OWNERSHIP

It's On You

Every meaningful change begins with a single, often uncomfortable truth: your life is your responsibility. The work you finish or avoid, the goals you pursue or postpone, the habits you strengthen or ignore. All of them belong to you. Ownership is not about blame; it is about agency. It is the recognition that while you cannot control every circumstance, you can always control your response. Procrastination thrives when you forget that. It feeds on the belief that your circumstances decide your actions. The moment you reclaim responsibility, you remove its fuel.

Procrastination is rarely about laziness. It is about resistance to discomfort. Taking ownership means facing that discomfort without excuses. When you say, "It's not my fault," you hand over your power to something else, such as your schedule, your boss, your past, your energy, or your environment. But when you say, "It's on me," you pull that power back where it belongs. Ownership is not a burden; it is freedom. It reminds you that your choices, not your conditions, shape your direction.

Every time you delay something important, you experience a split between intention and action. You know what needs to be done, but you avoid it, hoping that avoidance will make the discomfort disappear. It never does. What disappears instead is your trust in yourself. Ownership closes that gap. It says, "I will do this, not because it is easy, but because it matters, and because I said I would." This shift is not dramatic at first, but it is decisive. Each time you follow through, you rebuild self-respect. The same energy once spent defending excuses becomes energy for deliberate action.

Owning your actions requires honesty. You must see how your choices, and not chance, create your outcomes. That means acknowledging your patterns of delay. When do you avoid responsibility? What stories do you tell yourself to justify it? Perhaps you tell yourself you need to feel inspired first, or that the timing is not right, or that someone else is the reason you cannot begin. Each of these is a story that protects your comfort at the cost of your progress. The moment you recognise that pattern, you can interrupt it. Ownership begins with awareness.

Awareness deepens through reflection. Instead of rushing to fix everything at once, look closely at how avoidance shapes your days. Notice how often hesitation turns small tasks into sources of tension. Observe how the relief of postponing quickly turns into guilt or anxiety. This is not about judgment; it is about the connection between cause and effect. When you see clearly that your decisions produce your discomfort as well as your success, you stop trying to escape responsibility and start using it as leverage.

The language you use with yourself reveals your relationship with responsibility. When you say, "I have to," you create pressure. When you say, "I choose to," you create control. The difference is profound. One frames action as a demand; the other frames it as a decision. Ownership grows through this kind of language. Replace "I can't" with "I haven't yet." Replace "I'll try" with "I will." These adjustments may seem small, but they rewire how your mind perceives effort. They shift focus from limitation to possibility, from powerlessness to participation.

This mindset shift is not only motivational, it is practical. People who take ownership respond differently to setbacks. Instead of saying, "That's just the way things are," they ask, "What can I do differently next time?" They analyse, adapt, and move forward. Failure becomes feedback. Each experience, even a disappointing one, becomes a data point that strengthens strategy rather than a verdict that defines worth. Ownership converts mistakes into lessons and lessons into growth. Without it, you remain in the loop of waiting; for better conditions, for permission, for someone else to act first.

To build ownership, begin with reflection and small commitments. Start by noticing one area where you frequently delay. Ask what it costs you, perhaps stress, opportunity, peace of mind, and write it down. Then define one small action you can take today to reclaim that responsibility. The goal is not to transform overnight; it is to create proof that your choices matter. Each completed action, however minor, reinforces that truth. The next decision becomes easier because your mind has evidence that effort produces results.

Celebrate these moments of follow-through. Many people wait for monumental success to feel proud, but confidence is built from accumulated evidence of reliability. Each time you act when you could have avoided, you demonstrate that you can be counted on, even by yourself. That is the essence of integrity: doing what you said you would do, even when no one else is watching. Over time, this integrity becomes strength. It creates a kind of peace that no external achievement can replace.

Taking ownership also changes how you interact with others. You stop outsourcing accountability. You communicate with clarity, admit mistakes without defensiveness, and give credit without resentment. People who take responsibility attract trust, because reliability is magnetic. It signals maturity, the ability to navigate life without waiting for rescue or recognition. The more you practice it, the more you realise that ownership is not about perfection but persistence. It is not about having everything under control but about continually choosing to engage rather than retreat.

At its deepest level, ownership is self-leadership. It is the internal decision to stop living as a passenger in your own life. The world will always offer distractions, excuses, and reasons to delay, but none of them have authority unless you grant it. When you act from ownership, you no longer need to feel ready to move. You move because it is your responsibility to do so. You learn, you adjust, and you keep going. This is how progress compounds, through deliberate, accountable motion repeated over time.

You have more control than you think. Your choices write the story you live. When you stop negotiating with excuses and start taking responsibility for both your successes and your setbacks, procrastination loses its foothold. You begin to see that effort is not something imposed on you—it is something chosen by you. And choice, consistently exercised, is the foundation of freedom.

You cannot delegate ownership. You can only claim it. The moment you do, every task, challenge, and opportunity begins to look different. You no longer wait for conditions to align. You create alignment by showing up. Ownership does not eliminate struggle; it transforms it into meaning. It reminds you that the direction of your life will always come down to a single, powerful truth: it's on you.

ജ്ഞ

9

DESIGN FOR ACTION

You can have clarity of purpose, discipline of mind, and ambition in abundance, yet if your environment is cluttered or chaotic, even simple actions will feel like a struggle. The spaces in which you think, work, and live are not neutral. They either support your progress or undermine it. Every surface, sound, and object in your surroundings speaks to your brain, shaping how you focus and how you act. When you design your environment with intention, you make progress the path of least resistance. You stop fighting your surroundings and start being supported by them.

Most people assume procrastination begins within the mind, but often it begins outside it. The constant buzz of notifications, the pile of unfinished papers, the visual noise of too many open tabs. Each one pulls a fraction of your attention away from what matters. Your brain must filter and refocus with every distraction, losing clarity and burning energy that could have gone toward meaningful work. Over time, this friction compounds into fatigue and avoidance. The first step to overcoming procrastination is not always to try harder; it is to make it easier to begin.

Designing for action starts with subtraction. Remove what is unnecessary before you try to add anything new. Clear the surfaces where you work. Close the digital tabs that no longer serve you. Reduce the tools you keep to only what you use. The brain thrives on simplicity. A clean space does not guarantee clarity, but it makes clarity possible. When you sit down to focus, your environment should already be whispering permission to begin. Every object in sight should serve a purpose or stay out of the way.

Distraction rarely feels dramatic. It creeps in through small habits, such as checking a phone between tasks, leaving messages open, and glancing at irrelevant work. Each of these tiny leaks divides your attention and makes progress harder to sustain. The solution is to design friction into distraction and ease into focus. Keep your phone in another room when working. Disable notifications except for what is essential. Use a single workspace for deep work and nothing else. The mind follows cues. When your environment signals focus, your attention obeys.

Your space should not only remove obstacles but also invite engagement. Light, air, and movement matter more than people realise. Dim lighting dulls alertness. Poor posture drains energy. A stagnant body signals fatigue to the mind. Open a window, adjust your chair, or take a brief walk before beginning. These small physical adjustments create a shift in mental state. When the body feels ready, the mind follows. Comfort is not indulgence. Sustained attention is built through intentional effort and rest.

Sound is another force that shapes focus. The modern environment hums with invisible noise: the buzz of conversation, the ping of devices, the distant hum of traffic. Even when you think you can ignore it, your nervous system cannot. Constant background noise keeps the body slightly tense and the mind half-alert. If you can, seek silence. If you cannot, create controlled sound, steady, neutral background tones that support concentration. You do not need total isolation; you need consistency. Predictable sound is easier for the mind to ignore than irregular noise.

The layout of your environment should reflect your priorities. The tools you use most often should be within easy reach. The work that matters most should have a dedicated space. The act of setting up a workspace each day is not just logistical, but also psychological. When your environment mirrors your goals, starting becomes instinctive. The space itself becomes a trigger for action. Over time, the repeated association between place and purpose becomes automatic. You enter, and focus begins.

Routines strengthen this effect. Begin and end your work in the same way each day. Close your workspace when you are done so that it greets you fresh the next morning. Even a brief ritual, such as clearing the desk, opening the same document, or writing one intention for the session, creates continuity. You are teaching your brain to recognise the start of effort and to settle into it more quickly. These cues reduce hesitation. The environment, not just your willpower, carries the rhythm of your work.

Designing for action also requires awareness of the digital spaces you inhabit. The boundaries between work and distraction are often blurred by screens. Every open tab and notification invites a mental detour. Treat your digital workspace as carefully as your physical one. Keep a single window open for focused work. Organise your files and tools so you can find what you need without friction. Declutter your digital life with the same intention you bring to your desk. Focus is not born of willpower but of design.

The goal of an intentional environment is alignment. Your surroundings should reflect the life you are trying to build, not the noise you are trying to escape. Each design choice, from lighting to layout, is a form of self-respect. It says that your work, your focus, and your peace of mind are worth protecting.

When you enter a space that supports your goals, you feel it immediately. There is less internal argument, less negotiation. The next step feels obvious. You begin without strain, because the conditions are already working with you. This is what it means to design for action: to create an environment so aligned with your intentions that doing the right thing becomes the easiest thing.

Procrastination thrives in disorder; progress thrives in clarity. The state of your surroundings shapes the state of your mind. When you choose to design your world deliberately, you make momentum your default. You stop waiting for the perfect mindset, because your environment builds it for you. And once that happens, starting is no longer a battle.

ജ്ജ

10

FACE THE REAL ENEMY

Fear

At the heart of procrastination lies not laziness or distraction but fear. Fear wears many disguises: hesitation, perfectionism, indecision, self-doubt. It tells you that waiting is wise, that preparation is progress, and that someday you will feel ready. But readiness does not come from waiting. It comes from action. Fear convinces you that safety lies in postponement, when in truth, the longer you wait, the more intimidating the task becomes. To overcome procrastination, you must learn to face fear.

Fear is not the enemy itself; it is information. It signals that something matters, that an outcome carries weight, that the work ahead asks something real of you. The problem arises when you mistake that signal for a stop sign. Instead of moving toward what feels uncertain, you retreat, telling yourself you will return later, when you feel stronger. Yet fear does not fade with distance; it grows. Each delay feeds it. Each postponement turns anxiety into a habit. The only way to shrink fear is to confront it through action. You cannot think your way out of fear, but you can act your way through it.

The fear of failure is the most familiar form. You worry that beginning will expose your limits, that your best effort will fall short, that others will see your imperfections. This fear often hides behind refinement and perfectionism, the endless polishing that protects you from the vulnerability of release. But perfect is not the goal. Progress is. Perfection belongs to theory; movement belongs to reality. The courage to start imperfectly will always take you further than the fantasy of flawless beginnings.

Equally paralysing is the fear of judgment. You hesitate because you imagine the opinions of others; what they might say, how they might react, whether they might disapprove. But judgment is constant and unpredictable. It changes with time, perspective, and taste. To base your action on the avoidance of criticism is to give your power away. Those who accomplish meaningful work do not wait for universal approval. They move despite uncertainty, trusting that contribution matters more than perfection. When your focus shifts from impressing others to fulfilling your own standards, fear loses much of its leverage.

There is also the fear of success, the one most people overlook. Success carries responsibility. It changes expectations. It demands consistency. Some hesitate not because they doubt their ability to succeed, but because they fear what success will require next. They worry that they will not be able to sustain it or that the new version of themselves will be held to a higher standard. But growth is not a trap; it is a transition. You do not need to be ready for every future demand. You only need to handle the next one. Each success expands your capacity.

The way to master fear is not to wait for courage to arrive fully formed, but to act while it is incomplete. Courage is motion through uncertainty. It is the decision to begin while afraid and to discover strength within the act itself. Each time you confront fear, you gather evidence that it can be faced. That evidence becomes confidence. Confidence is not the absence of fear, but the proof that fear no longer controls you.

Understanding the mechanics of fear helps disarm it. Fear amplifies imagined consequences while obscuring real ones. You picture failure vividly but overlook the cost of inaction; the opportunities missed, the skills undeveloped, the confidence unearned. The pain of trying and falling short is temporary; the pain of never trying endures. When you shift your focus from what you might lose to what you inevitably lose by doing nothing, action begins to feel less risky and more necessary.

Fear thrives in vagueness. When a task feels undefined, the mind fills the gaps with threat. Clarity weakens fear because it replaces the unknown with structure. Break large goals into smaller, visible steps. Define what progress looks like today, not in the abstract future. A task you can see clearly is a task you can start. Every concrete step taken dissolves a portion of anxiety. Movement brings reality into view, and reality is rarely as frightening as imagination.

Perspective is the final antidote. When you view fear as an obstacle, it dominates your thinking. When you view it as a companion, it becomes manageable. Every meaningful pursuit will evoke discomfort. That discomfort is the price of growth, not the sign of danger. The people who accomplish what they set out to do feel fear as well; they just refuse to interpret it as a reason to stop. The difference between those who act and those who avoid is not bravery but interpretation.

Each time you act in the presence of fear, you reclaim power from it. Each time you finish something you once avoided, you train your mind to trust your ability to move through uncertainty. Over time, fear becomes familiar. It still appears, but it no longer dictates your pace. What once felt like resistance begins to feel like a signal that you are working on something meaningful.

Fear will always exist at the edge of your growth. That is its natural place. But it is not a barrier; it is a threshold. You cross it each time you start before you are ready, speak when your voice trembles, or take the next step without a guarantee. This is how courage is built, not in the absence of fear, but in the choice to move forward while it remains.

When you stop waiting for fear to disappear, you stop waiting for life to begin. Progress does not belong to the fearless; it belongs to the willing. Each act of courage, no matter how small, reclaims a piece of freedom from hesitation. And with enough repetition, you learn the most liberating truth of all: fear will visit, but it does not stay. It only has power if you offer it shelter.

ꟸ

11

EMOTIONAL PROCRASTINATION

When Avoidance Isn't Laziness

Not all procrastination comes from distraction or poor time management. Sometimes it is rooted in something, but far more powerful: emotion. Emotional procrastination is not the refusal to act; it is the attempt to avoid how action makes you feel. It is what happens when the mind postpones a task not because it is difficult, but because the emotions attached to it: fear, guilt, shame, uncertainty, feel heavy. You delay, not to save time, but to protect yourself from discomfort. The mind seeks safety in avoidance, and for a short while, it finds it. But what begins as self-protection soon becomes self-sabotage.

This form of procrastination hides in plain sight. It wears the mask of exhaustion, indecision, or perfectionism. You might tell yourself you are too tired, that the timing is wrong, or that you need to be in a better mood before you can begin. Yet beneath those explanations lies an emotional truth: perhaps the fear of being judged, the memory of a past failure, or the pressure to meet an impossible standard. The delay feels logical because the emotion feels real. But in protecting yourself from those feelings, you also block your growth. Avoidance does not erase emotion; it buries it alive. Each postponement reinforces the belief that discomfort must be escaped, and over time, the very thought of beginning becomes a trigger for anxiety.

The brain interprets uncertainty as danger, and emotional discomfort activates the same survival circuits as physical threat. When a task feels loaded with pressure or potential failure, your nervous system shifts into defence mode. It urges you to seek relief, which might look like organising your workspace, refreshing your inbox, or scrolling for inspiration. These diversions are not random; they are emotional anaesthetics. They provide momentary calm, but that calm comes at a cost. The longer you avoid the source of tension, the more powerful it becomes in your mind. A task left undone starts to grow in psychological weight, and soon even thinking about it feels exhausting.

At the centre of emotional procrastination is identity. You delay most on the tasks that challenge how you see yourself. You hesitate to write the proposal because it might expose a weakness. You avoid giving feedback because it risks rejection. You postpone pursuing an opportunity because success might force you to sustain a higher standard. You tell yourself you are waiting for the right conditions, but what you are truly waiting for is the feeling of safety that may never come. The fear is not about the task itself, but what it says about you. When self-worth becomes tangled with performance, every step forward feels like a test of character.

To break this pattern, awareness must come first. The next time you catch yourself delaying, pause long enough to ask: "What am I feeling right now?" You might uncover fear, embarrassment, frustration, or simply overwhelm. Naming the emotion separates it from the task. It reminds you that the feeling is not the work; it is just your body's signal of discomfort. Once you can name it, you can work with it instead of under it. This small moment of awareness marks the shift from emotional reaction to conscious choice.

Acceptance is the next step. Most people try to outthink their emotions, convincing themselves to feel better before they act. But emotional resistance grows stronger the more you fight it. The goal is not to erase discomfort but to allow it to exist without control. You can say, "I feel anxious, but I can still begin," or "I feel uncertain, but I can take one small step." This approach retrains the nervous system to see effort as safe. Over time, you stop associating emotional tension with danger, and action becomes easier to initiate.

Progress in emotional work often comes through small, deliberate movement. Big leaps trigger resistance, but small, specific steps slip beneath the threshold of fear. Write one sentence, send one message, make one decision. Each act of completion becomes proof that emotion and action can coexist. The mind learns that anxiety does not need to vanish before progress can begin. You realise that the hardest part of any task was not the doing, but the emotional negotiation that preceded it.

Environments that punish mistakes make emotional procrastination worse. When you treat errors as evidence of inadequacy, you turn every attempt into a referendum on your worth. The fear of being wrong outweighs the possibility of being right. Redefine success as honest engagement rather than flawless performance. The person who acts with imperfect effort will always outpace the person who waits for perfection. The aim is not to eliminate error but to grow through it. Progress made with imperfection is progress nonetheless, and the confidence it builds is grounded, not fragile.

Self-compassion is essential in this process. Harsh self-talk fuels emotional avoidance. The more you criticise yourself for hesitating, the more shame attaches to action, and the cycle deepens. Replace judgment with curiosity. Ask not "What is wrong with me?" but "What is this feeling trying to protect me from?" Maybe it is guarding your sense of competence, your need for rest, or your desire for control. When you respond with understanding instead of condemnation, you reclaim the mental space to move forward. Compassion is not leniency. It removes emotional noise and replaces it with calm focus.

As emotional awareness deepens, avoidance begins to lose its edge. You start to see that emotion is not an obstacle but a form of information. Fear reveals where growth lies. Guilt shows where values are misaligned. Frustration signals where expectations exceed resources. When you listen to emotion instead of fleeing from it, you discover the wisdom beneath the discomfort. The goal is not to suppress emotion, but to integrate it, to act with awareness.

Emotional procrastination is most powerful when it hides in the dark. Once you bring it into awareness, it begins to dissolve. The emotions that drive avoidance, fear, shame, and self-doubt are not permanent forces. They are weather systems that pass when you stop resisting them. Each time you act while carrying discomfort, you teach yourself a deeper truth: emotion and action can coexist. You do not need to wait for calm to begin. Calm is what follows movement, not what precedes it.

Avoidance may feel safe in the short term, but it comes at the cost of vitality. The energy you spend resisting emotion is the same energy you could use to create, connect, and progress. Acting through discomfort is not about pushing harder; it is about trusting that you can survive what you feel. The moment you do, avoidance loses its grip, and effort begins to feel less like struggle and more like liberation.

Emotional procrastination does not mean you are lazy or unmotivated; it means you are human. The emotions that once stopped you can become signals guiding you forward if you learn to interpret them correctly. Each time you begin despite unease, you strengthen your capacity for courage. Over time, you no longer wait for the right mood because you understand that emotion is not the gatekeeper of progress. The act of beginning itself is what steadies the mind.

When you stop running from what you feel, you stop running from what you can become. Every step you take in the presence of emotion is an act of strength. It is proof that you can meet yourself honestly and still move forward. And that, more than anything, is how emotional procrastination finally loses its power.

ഌ

12

PROGRESS OVER PERFECTION

Progress is not about sudden breakthroughs or flashes of inspiration. It is about the accumulation of small, deliberate acts that move you forward, even when no one notices. The people who grow, who build, who create lasting work are rarely the ones who wait for ideal conditions or perfect clarity. They are the ones who return to the work again and again, shaping it a little better each time. Perfection, for all its allure, freezes movement. It whispers that effort is only valuable when it looks flawless, that you must wait until every variable aligns before you begin. But waiting for perfection is how progress dies in silence. You do not grow through flawless execution; you grow through practice, through the willingness to act before you feel ready, and through the humility to learn while in motion.

Perfectionism wears the mask of care. It convinces you that hesitation is preparation, that the delay is strategic, that holding back is proof of your standards. Yet behind that careful restraint hides fear; the fear of imperfection, of judgment, of exposure. You tell yourself that one more draft will make it easier, one more day will make it safer, one more round of research will make it certain. But each moment spent waiting teaches your mind that safety lies in avoidance, not in effort. Over time, that lesson becomes instinct. Beginning feels dangerous because you have practised hesitation more than action. The truth is that clarity never precedes motion; it follows it. The first attempt, however awkward, always reveals more than another hour of deliberation. Progress is discovery, and discovery requires risk.

Momentum thrives on simplicity. When your goals are too large or abstract, the mind cannot find a place to begin. Vague intentions like "finish the project" or "get organised" leave no clear entry point, and the absence of definition breeds delay. But when you decide on one concrete task, such as writing one paragraph, making one call, or organising one folder, you reduce the friction between intention and action. Each completed task generates a small surge of energy, a confirmation that effort works. That evidence, repeated daily, becomes self-reinforcing. You no longer depend on bursts of motivation to start; you start because you trust the pattern that progress will always bring energy with it.

Small daily wins carry extraordinary power because they shift identity. You begin to see yourself not as someone waiting for the right conditions but as someone who creates them. Each act of completion rewires how you perceive challenge. A finished paragraph becomes proof that you can write. A cleared workspace becomes proof that you can organise. These fragments of proof accumulate until belief in your own reliability outweighs the fear of failure. Over time, this confidence becomes a kind of discipline that requires less negotiation.

You stop asking whether you are ready to begin. You begin because you have trained yourself to associate movement with relief.

The antidote to perfection is rhythm. When you work in small, repeatable cycles of effort and reflection, you begin to turn progress into a habit. Each cycle closes the gap between your current ability and your ideal. Reflection is what keeps that process intelligent. Without it, progress can become mechanical. When you pause at the end of each day to notice what worked, what didn't, and what might improve tomorrow, you start to see effort as data. You stop judging yourself for missteps and begin studying them. The smallest adjustments, like a clearer plan, a workspace, and an earlier start, can turn inconsistency into momentum. This rhythm, not perfection, is what sustains mastery over time.

Acknowledgement turns that rhythm into fuel. Many people accomplish more than they realise but feel perpetually behind because they never stop to recognise what they've already done. The absence of acknowledgement dulls the sense of reward that makes sustained effort possible. Taking a moment to notice your progress, whether through a note in a journal, a walk, or a brief pause to breathe, anchors achievement in memory. That moment of gratitude is not self-congratulation; it is calibration. It reminds your nervous system that work leads to satisfaction, not endless striving. The mind learns to crave the feeling of completion over the illusion of perfection, and that craving keeps you in motion.

Over time, progress itself becomes a philosophy. You start to measure success not by how flawless the outcome looks, but by how aligned your effort feels. A single hour of honest, focused work on what matters most can be more meaningful than a week of scattered productivity. When your actions serve your values, even small steps feel significant. You no longer chase validation or compete with other people's timelines. You begin to move with steadiness, knowing that growth unfolds at the pace of sincerity, not speed. Progress, in this sense, is less about performance and more about coherence, the alignment between what you say you want and how you actually live.

Perfection is brittle because it depends on control. It collapses the moment reality intrudes. Progress endures because it adapts. It accepts error as feedback and imperfection as part of creation. To value progress over perfection is to trade judgment for curiosity, to replace paralysis with participation. You begin to see that mastery is not a single achievement but an evolving relationship with effort. The best work you ever produce will not appear because you waited for the perfect idea. It will emerge because you kept refining the imperfect one.

Progress is not measured by how quickly you move but by how faithfully you return. You will have days of ease and days of resistance, moments of clarity and hours of fog. What matters is not consistency in emotion, but consistency in return. Each time you come back to the work, you reaffirm your direction. Each return strengthens your capacity to begin again. That is what dissolves procrastination, not the elimination of fear, but the steady practice of movement in its presence.

When you stop chasing perfection, you reclaim the freedom to improve. You stop living under the weight of imagined expectations and start engaging with the work in front of you. The act of progress becomes its own reward: tangible, grounded, alive. You realise that the measure of success is not whether today was flawless, but whether today was honest. The mind finds peace not in reaching perfection, but in knowing it moved closer to something meaningful. Each small advance, each imperfect completion, each honest attempt builds the confidence that tomorrow you can do it again. That is how progress becomes the antidote to delay, one step, one choice, one day at a time.

ꕤ

13

WINNING DAILY

Micro Habits & Goals

Progress does not depend on grand gestures or bursts of inspiration. It depends on what you do today. Big goals define direction, but small actions create momentum. The simplest way to prove to yourself that you can achieve something is to do it, not occasionally, but daily. Every completed task, no matter how small, builds evidence that you can act, decide, and follow through. Each daily win strengthens belief in your own reliability, and that belief is the foundation of confidence.

Winning each day is not about doing everything. It is about doing what matters most, consistently. The mind thrives on focus and closure, not chaos and overwhelm. When you reduce your day to one meaningful goal, that single task that, if completed, makes the day feel purposeful. The task does not need to be large; it simply needs to be clear. Finishing one deliberate act gives you more control than juggling ten that remain incomplete. The completion itself becomes a form of energy.

Procrastination often begins when the mind stares too far ahead. The vision is vast, the distance uncertain, and the steps in between undefined. The result is paralysis. But when you break the larger goal into clear, manageable steps, the impossible becomes approachable. Instead of facing a mountain, you face the next stone. Writing 300 words, organising one drawer, sending one proposal, each task feels small enough to begin but meaningful enough to matter. The mind stops defending itself from failure and starts engaging with what it can handle now.

Micro habits are the framework that makes this approach sustainable. They anchor your day in consistency and simplicity. A good micro habit is small enough to complete even on a difficult day, yet valuable enough to create momentum. Over time, these small acts compound, teaching you to trust yourself again. Each completion rewires your brain to associate effort with progress rather than exhaustion. Slowly, you stop waiting for motivation and begin moving because movement itself feels natural.

Here are a few examples of micro habits that build momentum without overwhelm:

- **Start your day with intention.** Write down one task that, if completed, will make the day feel successful. Keep it visible.
- **Use a five-minute rule.** When resistance appears, commit to just five minutes of action. Most of the time, momentum takes over.

- **End each day with closure.** Review what you finished, no matter how small, and identify one priority for tomorrow.
- **Simplify your setup.** Before starting, clear your workspace of distractions and open only what serves the task at hand.
- **Create a transition ritual.** A small, repeatable cue, like making tea, adjusting the lights, or playing instrumental music, signals your mind that it is time to work.
- **Practice one act of order.** Tidy your desk, organise a file, or clean a small space. Physical clarity supports mental clarity.

These habits are not complex, but their consistency builds identity. Each repetition tells your mind, *I am someone who follows through*. That belief grows stronger than hesitation. You begin to see discipline not as an effort of willpower, but as an expression of who you are becoming.

The same principle applies to daily goals. Instead of vague intentions like "be productive" or "work on the project," define success in specific, measurable terms. The brain responds to clarity; it resists ambiguity. Try setting goals like:

- Write 300 words for the article.
- Draft the first slide of the presentation.
- Spend 20 minutes studying a single concept.
- Review and reply to five important emails.
- Walk for fifteen minutes after lunch.

The goal is not to complete everything, but to complete something with intention. Each day becomes a self-contained victory that feeds into the next. You are not chasing transformation; you are building proof.

Reflection amplifies this process. When you end your day with a short review, what worked? What didn't? What small improvement can I make tomorrow? The reflection keeps you aware, steering habits away from autopilot and toward purpose. Over time, you begin to notice patterns in your energy and focus. You learn when you work best, how much effort different tasks truly require, and where you tend to drift. This awareness makes your effort more intelligent, less forced.

Acknowledgement transforms it all into fuel. Most people move quickly past their progress, measuring themselves only by what remains undone. Yet taking a moment to recognise what you accomplished is not indulgence; it is reinforcement. When you pause to note a win, however small, you remind your nervous system that effort is rewarded with satisfaction, not exhaustion. That satisfaction creates a craving for continuity. Progress becomes its own motivation.

Micro habits and daily goals do more than organise your day. They reshape how you see yourself. They bridge the gap between intention and identity. Each small act aligns your behaviour with the person you aspire to be, until the two are no longer separate. When you wake with a clear purpose and end the day with completion, you live inside a rhythm that sustains itself. The mountain may still exist, but you meet it one deliberate step at a time, with steady breath and unbroken momentum.

Progress built in this way is profound. It teaches you that transformation is not a leap but an accumulation, not a sudden change but a practised pattern. Each small victory builds the structure of consistency. Each reflection deepens understanding. Each acknowledgement renews the drive. You stop waiting for the right time because you realise it arrives every morning, when you choose to begin again.

ꟷ

14

THE MOMENTUM MINDSET

Momentum is the invisible current that turns effort into progress. It is what carries you forward when motivation fades and what keeps you steady when the path feels long. You cannot buy it, summon it on demand, or fake it with enthusiasm. Momentum must be built, and it is built through motion, through the discipline of beginning before you feel ready, and the consistency of returning even when the desire to continue has disappeared. Once momentum takes hold, it transforms the way work feels. Tasks no longer demand force; they pull you forward with their own gravity. Progress becomes less about willpower and more about flow.

Momentum begins in small, deliberate movement. Most people wait for clarity before they start, believing that understanding must come first. But action is what creates clarity. Each step you take reveals the next one. When you act, even imperfectly, you gather information that thinking alone could never produce. The mind learns best in motion. The difference between those who stay stuck and those who move forward is not the absence of fear or doubt, but the willingness to act in their presence. The first attempt may be uncertain, but it breaks the stillness that feeds hesitation. Once the cycle of movement begins, each completed action lowers resistance to the next.

Momentum also relies on rhythm. Progress is not made in constant acceleration but in cycles of push and recovery. The most consistent performers understand that movement does not have to mean exhaustion. They pace their energy so that effort feels sustainable, not desperate. When you create systems that allow you to begin easily and stop deliberately, you remove the drama from discipline. The start becomes automatic, the finish intentional. You stop burning out in bursts of intensity and instead build endurance through steadiness. In this rhythm, momentum is not something you chase; it is something you maintain.

The greatest threat to momentum is interruption. Distraction breaks the chain of continuity that progress depends on. Every time you abandon a task midstream, you pay a cognitive tax when you return. Your brain must rebuild the context it lost, reconnect the thread of thought, and re-establish focus. Protecting momentum, therefore, is an act of respect for your own attention. It means finishing what you begin before turning to what comes next. It means treating transitions as part of the work rather than breaks from it. It means designing your day so that you can flow from one state of focus to another without friction. When your environment and schedule align with this rhythm, continuity becomes effortless, and the quality of your work rises naturally.

Momentum grows stronger with completion. Each finished task creates a psychological loop that tells your mind the system works. It rewards you with a surge of confidence and relief, signalling that effort leads to resolution. The brain, always seeking efficiency, begins to crave that sensation of closure. You start to see effort not as a struggle but as a means to peace. The more cycles of completion you create, the easier it becomes to start the next one. Progress becomes habitual, not heroic. What was once a battle to begin becomes a rhythm you trust.

This is why momentum thrives on consistency more than intensity. Grand gestures create excitement, but repetition creates mastery. It is better to move steadily every day than to sprint sporadically. The accumulation of small, consistent effort builds a foundation that can bear weight over time. Even when results appear slow, the compounding effect of persistence cannot be overstated. Each repetition deepens the groove of discipline. Each day of action reinforces identity. The results may appear gradual, but they are exponential in their long-term impact.

Momentum is also sustained by perspective. When you interpret effort as punishment, every challenge feels heavier. But when you view effort as proof of progress, struggle becomes part of growth. The same action, reframed, generates a different emotional response. You are not "pushing through" work; you are advancing through it. Each repetition, each small victory, is a confirmation that you are shaping your future rather than waiting for it to shape you. Perspective transforms fatigue into purpose, and purpose sustains motion even when motivation wanes.

There will be times when momentum falters. Life disrupts routines, energy dips, and setbacks occur. The test is not whether you can avoid these interruptions, but how quickly you return after them. The most successful people are not those who never lose focus but those who recover it fastest. When momentum breaks, do not analyse endlessly; restart gently. Shrink your effort until it becomes manageable, and move. A single act of renewal, like a walk, an email sent, a page written, is often enough to reignite the chain of progress. The moment you act, inertia weakens. The moment you persist, momentum rebuilds.

In this way, momentum is both cause and effect. It is created by action and sustained by the belief that progress is possible. Each movement forward strengthens the conviction that another is within reach. You learn to trust the process more than the outcome. You stop measuring success by how far you have left to go and start valuing the simple fact that you are still in motion. Over time, that steadiness becomes power. You move not because you must but because it feels unnatural not to.

Momentum is not a gift for the motivated; it is the reward for the consistent. It grows in those who act even when enthusiasm fades, who return after they falter, and who finish what they start. When you adopt this mindset, progress becomes self-generating. You no longer depend on inspiration or external pressure. You learn that movement itself is medicine—that every step, however small, carries the potential to restore focus, confidence, and strength.

In the end, momentum is not about speed. It is about continuity, the assurance that as long as you keep moving, direction can always be corrected, and effort can always be renewed. The power of momentum lies in its simplicity: begin, continue, and return. The rest will follow.

ꕥ

15

HOW TO KEEP GOING

Resilience & Renewal

Every meaningful pursuit will test your endurance. There comes a point when the first rush of excitement has faded, the results are still distant, and the work in front of you feels heavier than before. This is where most people stop. They mistake fatigue for failure, assume their effort has lost meaning, and let the momentum they built slip away. Yet this is also where real progress begins. The ability to continue, especially when inspiration has disappeared, is the difference between temporary effort and lasting achievement. Keeping going is not about force; it is about rhythm, perspective, and renewal.

Resilience does not mean pushing endlessly through exhaustion. It means learning how to bend without breaking, to recover without quitting, and to return without resentment. The resilient mind understands that strain is not a signal to stop, but a message to adjust. Every process of growth, whether in nature, art, or work, depends on cycles of stress and restoration. The same applies to you. You expand through effort, and you strengthen through recovery. If you try to skip either, progress collapses. True resilience is the capacity to sustain both.

The first step in building that capacity is acceptance. Every long journey will include plateaus, setbacks, and moments of uncertainty. When you expect this, you stop interpreting them as personal shortcomings. You understand that fatigue, distraction, and even doubt are not failures of character but natural phases of effort. The problem arises when you fight these phases instead of working with them. A professional runner knows that the midpoint of a race feels the hardest precisely because the end is not yet in sight. A writer knows that the middle chapters demand more patience than the first or last. Resilience grows when you recognise these moments as part of the rhythm, not interruptions of it.

Renewal is the partner of resilience. Without it, endurance turns into depletion. Renewal means finding deliberate ways to refill the energy you spend. Rest alone is not enough; renewal comes from meaningful restoration. It might be a walk outdoors that reconnects you with stillness, a conversation that reminds you why your work matters, or a review of what you've already accomplished. Renewal requires intention. When you schedule recovery as seriously as you schedule effort, your stamina expands. You stop treating energy as a dwindling resource and begin to treat it as something you can restore with care.

Momentum often falters not because the work is too difficult, but because meaning fades from view. When you lose sight of why you started, every obstacle feels heavier. Resilience is easier when anchored in purpose. Remind yourself not only what you are working toward, but also what you are working from; the values, convictions, or experiences that gave this path importance in the first place. Meaning transforms fatigue into patience. It turns obligation into investment. The same task that once felt draining begins to feel necessary again, because you see it as part of something larger than the moment's discomfort.

The discipline of finishing grows from this understanding. Finishing is not about speed or perfection; it is about follow-through. It is the commitment to carry your work to completion even when the excitement that began it has vanished. Every unfinished task leaks energy. It occupies space in the mind and weakens your trust in your own reliability. Completion closes that loop. It signals to the brain that the effort was worth it and that you are capable of bringing things to an end. This sense of closure fuels confidence and releases focus for what comes next. You cannot sustain progress if you are always starting anew; resilience requires the satisfaction of ending well.

Finishing well does not mean refusing to rest until the goal is reached. It means knowing when the work is truly complete and when perfection has become avoidance. The mind will always whisper that one more revision, one more adjustment, will make the result flawless. But perfection is not the goal of resilience. The discipline of finishing lies in choosing completion over endless refinement. You decide that progress matters more than polish, that growth matters more than applause. Each time you finish, you teach your mind that closure is possible and that forward motion deserves reward.

There will be days when even the thought of continuing feels too heavy. In those moments, reduce your focus to the smallest possible unit of progress. When your energy is low, shrink the task until it fits your current strength. Write one sentence, organise one idea, make one call. Resilience does not depend on the size of the step but on the refusal to stop stepping. Once you begin again, even in miniature, the act of movement restores your sense of capability. The path forward often rebuilds itself in the motion of your return.

To keep going is not to chase endless growth but to maintain a connection to your purpose, to your process, and to yourself. Renewal gives you the clarity to recognise when to push and when to pause. Resilience gives you the strength to do both without shame. Finishing gives you the satisfaction that allows the next beginning to feel lighter. These three together form the architecture of endurance. They turn persistence into wisdom rather than struggle.

The most powerful work is rarely done in a rush of motivation. It is built through the patient's rhythm of showing up, stepping back, and returning. When you master that rhythm, you stop fearing pauses, setbacks, or plateaus. You know how to meet them, how to draw energy from meaning, and how to rise when the cycle begins again. This is how progress becomes permanent. You keep going not because you never tire, but because you have learned how to renew.

16

THE ACCOUNTABILITY EFFECT

Discipline begins within, but it strengthens through connection. You can make promises to yourself in silence, but those promises are easy to bend and easier to forget. Left alone, the mind can rationalise almost anything: one more break, one more day, one more excuse disguised as self-care. But when you voice your intentions to someone else, when your goals become visible beyond your own imagination, something shifts. Accountability turns your intentions into living commitments. Once another person knows what you aim to do, the promise gains structure, weight, and consequence. It stops being a passing thought and becomes part of your character.

True accountability is not about guilt or external pressure. It is about alignment between what you say and what you do. It ties your private ideals to public reality and gives your choices a visible outline. When you tell someone you will deliver, the act of speaking transforms the abstract into something tangible. That promise now exists in the world, and the knowledge that it will be seen, measured, and remembered changes how you behave. You plan with more care, you act with more intention, and you recover faster from setbacks because your word is at stake. Accountability connects integrity to effort, and that connection breeds consistency.

Most people resist accountability because they mistake it for surveillance. They imagine it as someone watching over their shoulder, waiting for them to fail. But real accountability is not control. It works like a mirror, showing you what is actually happening instead of what you wish were happening. When you check in regularly with someone you trust, you gain a clearer view of your own habits: where you follow through, where you hesitate, where you fall into patterns of avoidance. That awareness is worth more than any external push because it replaces confusion with clarity. You begin to understand not just whether you're doing the work, but *how* you respond to resistance, pressure, and distraction.

Building accountability requires intention. It will not appear on its own. You must create the structures that make it real, structures that are steady enough to guide you but flexible enough to evolve with you. Choose someone who respects your goals, not someone who merely demands results. Accountability built on trust nurtures growth; accountability built on fear breeds resentment. The goal is to create an environment in which you can be honest about progress, setbacks, and effort without hiding behind excuses or guilt. The act of reporting what you've done, even imperfectly, keeps your focus alive. It transforms discipline from an isolated struggle into a shared process of improvement.

Accountability also sharpens clarity. Vague intentions, like "I'll try to do better," "I'll start soon," "I'll get to it when I have time", cannot hold you accountable because they cannot be measured. To be accountable, a goal must be specific enough to be tracked. When you define what you want to complete, how you'll measure it, and when you'll deliver it, you give accountability something to hold onto. Every check-in becomes a moment of recalibration. If you fall short, you analyse why. If you succeed, you recognise what worked. This rhythm of definition, action, and reflection transforms accountability from pressure into process. It becomes a natural part of how you manage progress rather than a punishment for when you fail.

The real power of accountability lies not in being observed but in being seen. When someone witnesses your effort, the messy beginnings, the slow progress, the steady return, it validates that the struggle itself has worth. Progress feels more real when it is shared, because human beings are wired for recognition. To have someone say, "I see you showing up," carries a strength that no internal pep talk can replace. It reminds you that your discipline contributes to something beyond personal achievement. It reinforces that your reliability benefits others, that your follow-through creates stability, trust, and momentum for those around you.

As accountability deepens, it evolves from external structure to internal compass. At first, you might need the reminder of a deadline, a mentor's question, or a peer's check-in to stay consistent. Over time, those external cues are internalised. You begin to anticipate them yourself. You no longer need to be asked, because the act of being accountable has shaped your sense of self. You want to deliver not because someone is waiting, but because you want to be the kind of person who follows through. Accountability, when practised over time, turns into integrity.

Still, accountability cannot thrive in isolation from empathy. To build it sustainably, you must allow room for imperfection. Progress is not linear, and even the most disciplined people falter. The purpose of accountability is not to shame you when you fall behind, but to help you return faster. That return, the ability to reset, to face the truth of where you are, and to begin again, is what defines resilience. When you can admit to another person that you slipped, without defensiveness or despair, you prove to yourself that mistakes are recoverable and that effort, not perfection, is the measure of consistency.

Accountability is strongest when it is shared. Find one or two people who are pursuing their own forms of growth, maybe different goals, but a similar respect for discipline. Create an exchange where both of you track and report your efforts, where you hold space for each other's successes and lapses without comparison or criticism. Over time, you will find that your energy stabilises through that connection. When your motivation wanes, their momentum can lift you. When theirs falters, your reliability can lift them. Mutual accountability transforms the lonely act of persistence into a communal rhythm. It replaces isolation with shared momentum.

Technology can support this process, but it cannot replace sincerity. A tracking app or calendar reminder can record what you plan to do, but it cannot inspire you to care. Accountability grows from a relationship, from the knowledge that someone genuinely expects your best and believes you are capable of it. Even a short weekly conversation with a peer or mentor can recalibrate your focus better than any digital notification. What matters most is not the frequency of contact but the quality of attention. When you know you will have to look someone in the eye and tell the truth about your week, you start managing your days differently.

The most important step in building accountability is consistency. It must be ongoing, not occasional. One check-in does not create change; rhythm does. Treat accountability as a practice rather than a remedy. Set a cadence for review, weekly, biweekly, and monthly, and keep it sacred. Over time, the act of returning becomes its own kind of fuel. Each check-in marks another cycle of effort, reflection, and renewal. The structure keeps you honest; the repetition keeps you grounded.

At its heart, accountability is a form of care, a care for your promises, for the people who rely on you, and for the person you are becoming. It is not about pressure or perfection. It is about respect for the connection between word and action. When you learn to honour that connection, procrastination begins to lose its comfort. You can no longer hide behind delay because you know delay affects more than your schedule; it shapes your integrity. Accountability transforms effort into character and intention into trust. It reminds you that progress is rarely a solo act. You grow best not in isolation, but in the presence of others who expect you to keep going, and who believe, even when you forget, that you can.

ꕥ

17

HELPING OTHERS (AND YOURSELF AGAIN)

Growth begins as a personal pursuit but sustains itself through connection. You can spend months building systems for focus, discipline, and consistency, but their strength is tested when you step beyond yourself, when you bring that discipline into the lives of others. Progress deepens when it stops being private. The act of helping someone else change the way they think, work, or believe reminds you of your own strength, and in doing so, renews it.

Procrastination often feels isolating. It thrives in secrecy, convincing you that you are the only one struggling to begin. Yet the moment you start speaking with others about their challenges, you discover the truth: everyone wrestles with resistance in some form. Fear of failure, fatigue, confusion, uncertainty, they're all universal. That realisation alone lightens the burden. What once felt like a personal flaw begins to look like a shared human pattern. And shared patterns are easier to confront than private shame.

Helping others creates an energy that solitude cannot generate. When you encourage a friend to start the project they've been avoiding, when you listen to a colleague describe their frustration and help them find a step forward, you engage your own dormant motivation. The clarity you offer to others begins to reflect on you. Advice that once sounded theoretical becomes something you must embody. You cannot genuinely tell someone to take action without confronting where you've been avoiding it yourself. In this way, support becomes a mirror for integrity. It compels you to live what you teach.

There is also a psychological rhythm that makes helping others powerful. When you guide someone through a problem you've faced, you shift from identification to perspective. Instead of drowning in your own obstacles, you begin to analyse them from the outside. You see patterns that were invisible when you were too close to your own resistance. Explaining how to break through procrastination, how to start small, how to manage fear, and how to stay consistent forces your mind to organise these ideas clearly, and that organisation transforms them into habits. Teaching a principle is the most effective way to internalise it.

Connection restores momentum because it reframes progress as a shared responsibility. When you are part of a group, a partnership, or even an informal circle of support, your effort stops being abstract. You are no longer working in isolation, where excuses echo unchallenged. You are part of a rhythm where your progress fuels someone else's, and theirs fuels yours. Even small exchanges, such as checking in, sharing updates, and acknowledging effort, generate accountability and belonging. The sense of "we're in this together" changes how you show up. Responsibility begins to feel less like pressure and more like purpose.

Helping others also sharpens empathy, and empathy strengthens resilience. When you listen to someone else describe the fear, doubt, or exhaustion that keeps them from moving forward, you begin to approach your own challenges with more compassion. You recognise that discipline does not require perfection; it requires patience. You stop treating your own delays as moral failures and start seeing them as part of a larger process of learning and adjustment. Supporting others softens your self-criticism, and that gentleness, paradoxically, makes it easier to act. A mind that feels safe to try is a mind that will move.

The act of lifting others creates emotional balance. Every time you offer perspective, motivation, or encouragement, you generate positive emotion in the process. The same brain circuits that light up when you receive support activate when you give it. Helping others is not just altruism; it is a neurochemical reset. It interrupts the self-focused loops of overthinking and replaces them with a sense of connection, competence, and contribution. In moments when your own motivation fades, helping someone else find theirs can reignite your own.

To sustain this, seek out or create spaces where mutual support is natural. You don't need a formal group or a grand structure, just consistency and sincerity. Reach out to a peer with similar ambitions and agree to share progress weekly. Join a community that values growth rather than perfection. Offer feedback where you can, and ask for it in return. The value lies less in the specific format and more in the presence of honest dialogue. Each exchange becomes a checkpoint, a small pause to realign your intentions with your actions.

Over time, you may notice that helping others refines not only your work habits but your outlook on success itself. It shifts your focus from competition to contribution. You begin to see growth not as a private climb but as a shared ascent. Your achievements no longer feel like isolated victories but like part of a collective upward motion. And that change in perspective, the move from "me" to "us", brings a steadiness. You stop measuring your worth solely by your own output and start valuing the progress you help to create in others.

Helping others is also a reminder that leadership is not a title but a practice. Leadership begins when you use your progress to illuminate someone else's path. It doesn't matter whether you lead a team, a peer, or a single friend. When you demonstrate consistency, honesty, and persistence, you permit others to do the same. The example you set often travels farther than your advice. You show that it's possible to move even when conditions aren't perfect, to persist even when enthusiasm fades, and to return even after delay. Each time you live that truth, you strengthen it, not only in others, but in yourself.

At its core, helping others is a form of renewal. It reconnects you to meaning when your own goals begin to feel routine or heavy. It reminds you that effort, at its best, is an act of service, that the discipline you cultivate is not only for personal gain but for the value it adds to the people around you. Contribution has a way of resetting perspective. It brings gratitude back into the process and converts fatigue into purpose.

Transformation was never meant to be solitary. You can make progress alone, but you sustain it together. Helping others doesn't dilute your focus; it strengthens it. It doesn't slow your growth; it multiplies it. The more you give, the more you clarify what truly matters, and the more grounded you become in the kind of person you are becoming. In helping others rise, you lift yourself again.

ꕥ

CONCLUSION

The Practice of Progress

Procrastination is not a flaw to fix but a language to understand. It speaks in hesitation, in distraction, in the small delays that feel harmless in the moment but grow into patterns over time. Learning to overcome procrastination is not about crushing resistance or forcing yourself into endless motion. It is about developing the awareness to recognise when you are avoiding, the patience to examine why, and the discipline to move anyway. Each time you turn intention into action, you are not simply finishing a task; you are rewriting the story you tell yourself about what you are capable of.

Progress begins the moment you stop waiting for ideal conditions. The perfect time, the perfect plan, or the perfect mood will never arrive. Readiness is not a gift that appears before action; it is a state you create through movement. Every time you begin before you feel prepared, you prove that uncertainty is survivable. You teach your mind that effort is not something to fear. Over time, this practice becomes its own form of confidence, a certainty that you can handle what needs to be done, even if you cannot yet see the entire path ahead.

The journey through this book has shown that procrastination has little to do with time and everything to do with emotion. It grows where fear is unexamined, where energy is neglected, and where vision is unclear. It thrives in the spaces between intention and motion. But once you begin to manage your energy, clarify your purpose, and take ownership of your choices, procrastination loses its authority. You stop treating it as an enemy to defeat and start seeing it as a signal, a reminder that something in your process needs care, not condemnation. Understanding this turns discipline into compassion and action into an act of alignment.

The four forces you have explored, vision, energy, focus, and ownership, form the foundation of steady, meaningful progress. Vision gives you direction. It transforms scattered ambition into a sense of purpose that sustains effort through uncertainty. Energy fuels that vision, giving you the endurance to continue even when motivation fades. Focus gathers that energy into precision, helping you direct it where it matters most. Ownership binds the entire process together, reminding you that no matter what happens, responsibility for your next step belongs to you. Together, these forces turn intention into movement and movement into growth.

But even the most disciplined individual cannot thrive in isolation. Accountability and connection transform these principles into practice. When you share your goals with others, when you support and are supported, you create an ecosystem of progress that is larger than your willpower. You learn that growth is not a solitary achievement but a shared rhythm. Encouraging others strengthens your own commitment because it reminds you of what you value. Seeing others persist reignites your own resilience. In the act of helping, you reinforce what you have learned, and in being helped, you remember that progress is not proof of independence; it is evidence of interdependence.

There will still be days when hesitation returns, when energy runs thin, and when the weight of unfinished work feels heavy. On those days, the goal is not perfection but recovery. Return to movement in the smallest way possible. Write one line, send one message, organise one small task. Every step, however minor, reclaims a piece of momentum. You cannot control every outcome, but you can control when you begin again. Consistency is not built through flawless performance but through the willingness to start over each time you stall. That willingness, repeated across days, becomes resilience.

The truth is that progress does not happen in leaps; it happens in layers. Each day of focused effort adds another layer to your confidence, another degree of trust in your ability to follow through. Each completed task reinforces your belief that discipline and peace are not opposites; they coexist. When you finish what you start, even in small ways, you silence the noise of avoidance and replace it with the calm of completion. You stop chasing productivity as an external measure of worth and begin to experience it as an internal alignment between what you intend and what you do.

As you continue beyond these pages, remember that the purpose of this work is not to perfect your schedule but to reclaim your agency. Procrastination feeds on powerlessness; it fades when you remember that choice is always within reach. You may not control how you feel, but you control what you do with those feelings. You may not control the conditions, but you control your response to them. The freedom to act is the freedom to lead your own life.

There will always be new challenges, new distractions, and new fears that tempt you to delay. But now you know that waiting never brings ease. Action does. The smallest step forward carries more strength than the most convincing excuse. When you choose to move despite uncertainty, you transform hesitation into progress. You reclaim your time, your focus, and your confidence through steadiness.

Progress is not a performance. It is a practice. It grows from how you show up when no one is watching, from how you recover after you stumble, from how you continue to choose movement when comfort calls you back. The power you seek has always been in the next step, the next attempt, the next decision to begin. There is no better time to reclaim it than now.

Every act of follow-through, every finished task, every moment of renewed focus is a declaration: you are capable of leading your life with purpose. The path ahead will still test you, but it will also keep teaching you. Momentum does not disappear; it waits for your return. Begin again. That is all progress ever requires.

ജ്ജ